Contents

Introduction

As the seasons change, you will see many differences in the plants and animals around you. Have fun keeping a nature diary, listen for the changing sounds throughout the year and look out for migrating birds. Paint sunflower pots, make pictures from autumn leaves and learn how you can help to keep animals warm in winter.

1 Look out for numbers like this. They will guide you through the step-by-step instructions for the projects and activities, making sure that you do things in the right order.

Further facts

Whenever you see this 'nature spotters' sign, you will find interesting facts and information, such as how far some animals migrate, to help you understand more about nature all year round.

discovering  nature

All Year und

lewitt

Franklin Watts
London • Sydney

An Aladdin Book
© Aladdin Books Ltd 2000
Produced by
Aladdin Books Ltd
28 Percy Street
London W1P 0LD

First published in Great Britain
in 2000 by
Franklin Watts Books
96 Leonard Street
London EC2A 4XD

ISBN 0-7496-3717-X (hardcover)
ISBN 0-7496-4608-X (paperback)

Editor: Kathy Gemmell

Consultant: Helen Taylor

Designer: Simon Morse

Photography: Roger Vlitos

Illustrators: Mike Atkinson & Simon Morse

Printed in the U.A.E.
A CIP catalogue record for this book
is available from the British Library.

Original design concept by David West Children's Books

Hints and tips

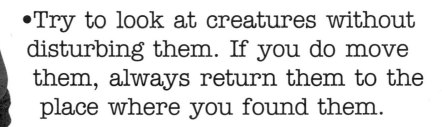

- Do not pick leaves or flowers from a plant. Only take ones that are already on the ground.

- Try to look at creatures without disturbing them. If you do move them, always return them to the place where you found them.

- Before touching soil or plants, cover any cuts with a plaster.

- Do not rub your face or eyes when working with plants or soil. Always wash your hands afterwards.

SOME BERRIES ARE POISONOUS

Wherever you see this sign, ask an adult to help you. Never use sharp tools or go exploring on your own.

Get an adult to help you

This warning sign shows where you have to take special care when doing a project. For example, when you look for wild berries, never eat any without asking an adult first. Some berries are poisonous and will make you very ill if you eat them.

Nature diary

Look and listen carefully and you will notice fascinating things happening in nature all year round. You can make a nature diary to keep a record of the things you spot at different times of year, both in the city and in the countryside.

Month by month

1 To make a nature diary, you will need a large pad, pen and pencils, glue and tape. Make a page for each month like the one in the picture.

2 Collect leaves and pine needles from the ground. Leave them to dry, then glue them into your diary. Make sure you label them.

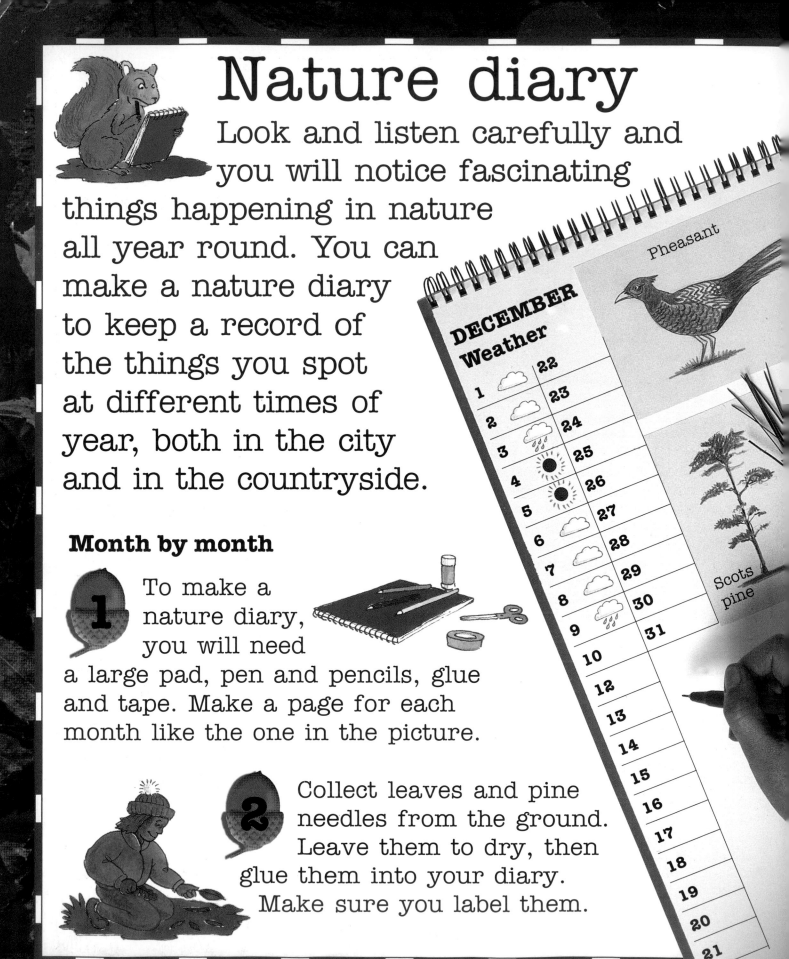

Pheasant

DECEMBER Weather

1	22
2	23
3	24
4	25
5	26
6	27
7	28
8	29
9	30
10	31
12	
13	
14	
15	
16	
17	
18	
19	
20	
21	

Scots pine

Fern

Scots pine needles

Oak tree

NOTES:
2nd Dec: - Saw four pheasants pecking in a field.

Puddles frozen

Frost on the grass, bare trees

Keeping records

You can keep records for your nature diary in many different ways. The more ways you use, the more interesting your diary will be.

Hang a thermometer outside and record the temperature each day. Write down the different things you spot on hot and cold days.

Make sketches. You might not remember what you have seen after you get back home. Glue the sketches into your diary.

If you have a camera, take photographs. You may notice something you didn't spot at first when you see the print.

3 Draw pictures and write notes about interesting things you see. Every day, copy one of the symbols below to show the weather.

Sunny	Cloudy	Rainy	Snowy	Stormy

Seasons

As spring turns to summer then to autumn and winter, the weather changes. Look out for changes in the landscape and in plants and animals during each season of the year.

Changing places

1 Choose a place that is easy for you to visit often. Try to find somewhere with a tree, plants and maybe a pond.

2 Paint a picture or take a photograph of the place you have chosen in every season. If you paint, copy the colours carefully.

3 Glue your pictures onto coloured card and label them with the right season. Spot the differences between your pictures.

Winter

Summ

All over the world

Each part of the world has its own kind of weather. Hot, dry places have different plants and animals from icy, cold places.

It is freezing all year at the poles. Few plants grow. Animals have thick coats and an extra layer of fat.

Tropical rainforests are warm and wet all year. Plants grow thick and fast and the forests teem with insects, birds and other animals.

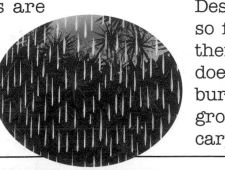

Deserts have little rain so few plants grow there. When rain does fall, flowers burst from the ground in a carpet of colour.

Window box

You can grow plants all year round even if you don't have a garden. Try planting herbs in a window box. When they have grown, pinch the leaves to smell the herbs' fragrance.

Indoors and outdoors

1 You will need packets of herb seeds and a window box with compost in it.

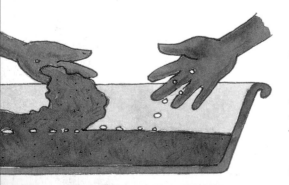

2 Sprinkle the seeds on the compost. Leave space between the different seeds. Lay more compost on top. Put the box on an indoor windowsill or, in spring or summer, outside.

4 When the herbs have grown, you can snip off the leaves to use for cooking. Only cut off what you need. The leaves will grow back again.

Herb garden

Herbs from a herb garden can be used for flavouring food, for brewing herbal teas and for treating illnesses.

Rosemary tea is good for soothing headaches and upset stomachs.

The leaves of chives give an onion flavour to salads.

Parsley stalks have a stronger flavour than the leaves.

Basil is grown among other plants to keep insects away. You can add its leaves to tomato dishes.

3 Water the herbs regularly. If they are outside, check that there has been enough rain.

Seasonal sounds

Go outside and listen carefully. Some sounds you hear are made by people or machines but others are noises made by nature. Make a note of all the natural sounds you can hear at different times of the year.

Listen closely

Nightingale

Jay

1 In the early spring, listen for male birds singing to attract a mate. Later, baby birds cheep noisily for food.

2 In the summer, insects buzz among the flowers and grasshoppers sing in the grass.

Fly

Grasshopper

Geese

Croaking frogs

In the spring, male frogs gather together in ponds and croak loudly. Each one is trying to attract a female to mate with. They can even croak underwater.

Frog

Air sack

3 In the autumn, listen for wings beating as flocks of geese fly south for the winter. In woods, listen for nuts falling into crunchy leaves.

When a frog croaks, a pouch of skin under its chin fills with air and helps the croaking sound to carry over a distance. Some frogs are named after the sounds they make, such as the snoring puddle frog, which is found in parts of Africa.

Chestnut

Rough ridges on the grasshopper's back legs rub against the wings to make a chirruping noise.

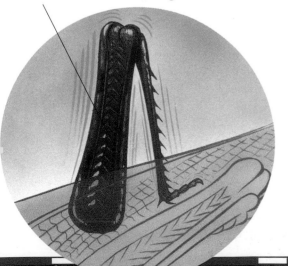

4 In winter, listen for the harsh caw of crows and rooks. They nest in the tops of trees and you can sometimes see them looking for food in rubbish tips.

Rook

Sunflowers

Sunflowers are very useful plants. Animals eat the leaves, yellow dye is made from the petals and oil is pressed from the seeds. Plant a sunflower seed in spring and by the summer it will have grown taller than you!

Painting and planting

1 You will need a packet of sunflower seeds, soil, three big flower pots and some paints.

2 Paint pictures of sunflowers on the outside of the pots. Plant two or three seeds in each pot. Water them regularly.

3 As the shoots appear, leave the strongest shoot in each pot to grow and pull up the others.

4 Your sunflowers will grow very tall. You can support the stems with garden canes.

Follow the Sun

Although sunflowers look like bright yellow Suns, they are called sunflowers for another reason. In the morning, they face the rising Sun. As the Sun moves throughout the day, the sunflowers turn their heads to follow it across the sky.

Noon

Morning

Evening

5 After the petals die, leave the flower heads for the birds. They will eat the seeds that form in the middle of the sunflower.

Butterflies and moths

Butterflies visit flowers in the daytime. Moths often feed at night. They use long feeding tubes like drinking straws to suck sweet juice called nectar from the flowers. Look for butterflies and moths when the flowers they feed on are in bloom.

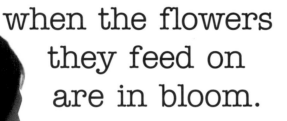

Butterfly watching

1 Butterflies are attracted to purple flowers with a strong scent, like buddleia flowers. Buddleia is also called the butterfly bush.

2 Make sketches and take notes of butterflies you see. This will help you look them up later in a field guide.

3 Use binoculars to help you spot butterflies. This will let you see their markings more clearly and will let you watch without disturbing them. You might even see some having a drink from a puddle.

Nectar eaters

Most butterflies live only for a short time in the summer when the flowers are out. Other creatures that drink nectar, such as hummingbirds, make long journeys to find flowers in bloom all year round.

Honeysuckle smells most strongly at night to attract moths.

Butterflies curl their feeding tubes under their heads when they are not in use.

Tiny Australian honey possums have long tongues to lick nectar from banksia flowers.

A hummingbird hovers in front of a flower while it sucks nectar with its long tongue.

Collections

Go for a walk at any time of year and you will find all kinds of interesting natural things. Make a collection for each season, or for places you visit like the park or the seashore.

NEVER TAKE EGGS FROM NESTS

Make a mini museum

1 Find a cardboard box with a good sized base. Cut down the sides to make a frame.

2 Line the box with coloured paper. This will be the background for your mini museum.

Get an adult to help you

Cockle shell

Garden snail shell

Chestnut

Chestnut husk

Maple leaf

Cedar cone

3 Arrange the objects you have collected in the box. Then carefully glue them down. Label each item clearly.

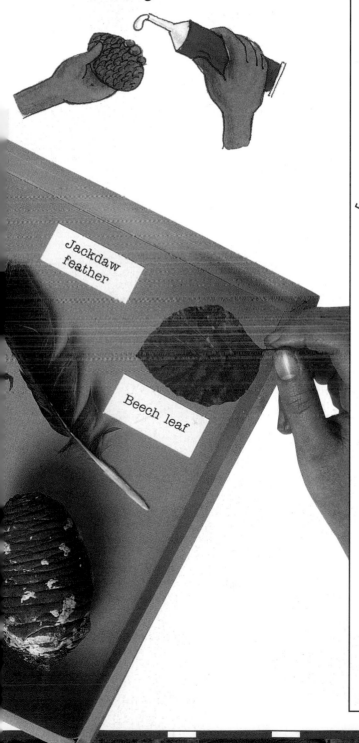

Jackdaw feather

Beech leaf

Flying feathers

Birds are the only creatures that have feathers. Their feathers are shaped for the different jobs they have to do. You can tell which part of a bird's body a feather comes from.

Small covert feathers make the front of the wing smooth.

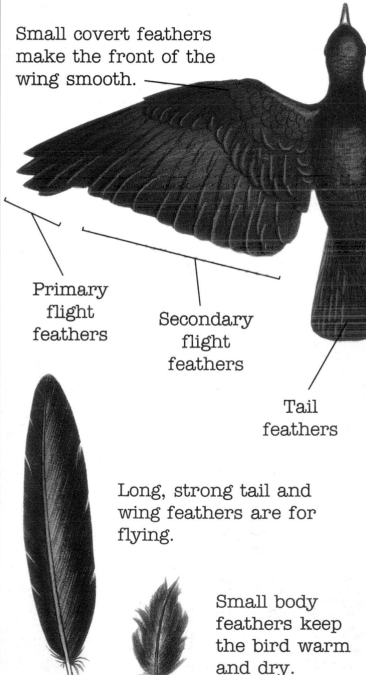

Primary flight feathers

Secondary flight feathers

Tail feathers

Long, strong tail and wing feathers are for flying.

Small body feathers keep the bird warm and dry.

Fruit

Fruit is the part of a plant that holds the seeds for a new plant to grow. When a flower dies, a fruit grows in its place. Tiny apples start to grow after apple blossom dies in the spring. By autumn, the apples are juicy and ready to eat.

Fruit salad

1 Make a delicious fruit salad with lots of different fruits. First, cut each fruit in half or into quarters.

2 Scoop or pick out any seeds you can see.

Look carefully at them through a magnifying glass. Remember which seeds come from which fruit.

Get an adult to help you

Wild berries

Wild berries are often bright and shiny. Birds spot them easily and swoop down to eat them. The birds then scatter plant seeds in their droppings, letting new plants grow.

In winter, bright red holly berries make a feast for hungry birds when there is little food about.

Mistletoe grows on the branches of other trees. Its white berries are poisonous to people and animals.

Blackberries grow wild on prickly brambles in early autumn. Birds, animals and people like to eat them.

SOME BERRIES ARE POISONOUS. ALWAYS ASK AN ADULT.

3 Ask a friend to match each seed to the fruit it came from.

Changing colour

Trees make food using the green colour in their leaves, called chlorophyll. In the summer, trees store the food they make. By autumn, the chlorophyll is not needed. It breaks down and turns the leaves red, brown, gold and orange.

Leaf pictures

1 Collect as many different autumn leaves as you can. Sort them into different shapes and colours.

2 You will need a clip frame and some coloured paper. Cut out a piece of paper the same size as the clip frame and lay it over the base of the frame.

Winter leaves

By winter, most of the fallen leaves will have rotted away. Only leaf skeletons, evergreen leaves and pine needles remain.

A leaf skeleton forms when the soft part of the leaf rots, leaving the tough stem and the veins.

Holly trees are evergreen. They keep their shiny, prickly leaves all year round.

Pine needles are very thin leaves that can survive the cold. They stay on the trees all winter.

3 Arrange the leaves into a pattern or a picture, then lay the glass on top. The glass will hold the leaves in position.

Get an adult to help you

Looking for food

In spring and summer, animals and birds can usually find plenty of food to eat. Many have to make long journeys to find enough food at other times of year. The journeys they make are called migrations.

Spot migrating birds

1 You can often identify birds by the way they behave or the way they fly. Before flying off, migrating swallows gather together on telephone wires.

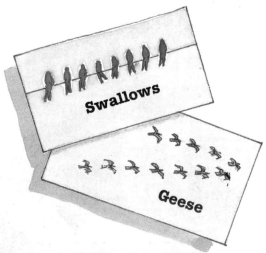

Swallows

Geese

2 Migrating geese fly off together in a V shape. Look out for geese and swallows in the autumn. Make picture cards to keep a record of all the migrating birds you spot.

Mexico

South America

Finding the way

Each year, animals, birds and insects find their way across thousands of kilometres of land and sea. Whales swim halfway around the world and caribou travel between the Arctic plains and northern forests. Match the coloured arrows to the arrows on the globe to see the migration routes.

➡ Humpback whales follow the coastline on their journey between cold polar and warm tropical seas.

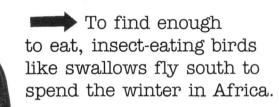

➡ To find enough to eat, insect-eating birds like swallows fly south to spend the winter in Africa.

➡ Caribou follow the same paths each year. They go south in the autumn and back north again in the spring.

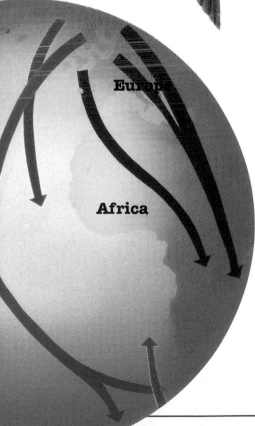

North Pole

Europe

Africa

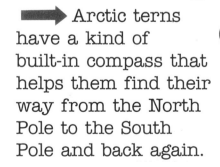

➡ Arctic terns have a kind of built-in compass that helps them find their way from the North Pole to the South Pole and back again.

➡ Monarch butterflies fly south from Canada in huge numbers, to spend the winter in Mexico.

Hibernation

In the winter, when there is very little food around, bears, bats, hedgehogs and dormice go into a long sleep called hibernation. They hide away in a safe, dry place and sleep until the warm spring weather wakes them up again.

The big sleep

1 Make an animal shelter in the autumn. Collect dry sticks and some straw and leaves for warm bedding.

NEVER DISTURB A HIBERNATING ANIMAL

2 In a quiet place outside, make a strong frame with the sticks. Cover it with earth, grass and leaves and put the bedding inside.

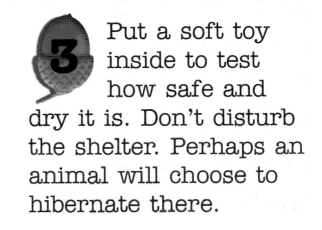

3 Put a soft toy inside to test how safe and dry it is. Don't disturb the shelter. Perhaps an animal will choose to hibernate there.

During the long winter sleep in her den, a mother bear wakes to give birth to her cubs.

Winter and summer

Some animals hibernate together in winter. Some sleep in summer when water is scarce. This summer sleep is called aestivation.

During the winter, some kinds of bats hibernate together. They hang upside down in enormous groups in sheltered caves.

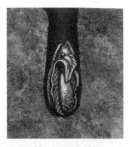

During the summer when their pools dry up, lungfish sleep in the mud. They use their lungs to breathe air.

Asleep in the soil

Just as some animals curl up and sleep all winter, bulbs are asleep too, buried in the soil. They wait for the warm spring weather to come before they start to grow. See how a hyacinth bulb will not grow in the dark but starts to grow shoots in the light.

Grow a bulb

1 Start this project in the autumn. You will need a hyacinth bulb, a jar and some toothpicks. Fill the jar nearly to the top with water.

2 Firmly stick four toothpicks in around the middle of the bulb. Balance the bulb in the top of the jar so its base is in the water.

3 Put the bulb in a dark cupboard. Check it occasionally to make sure it has enough water.

4 Before winter is over, bring the bulb out into the light. It will start to grow and you will soon have a beautifully scented hyacinth flower to enjoy.

Waiting to grow

Eggs, seeds and tubers, such as potatoes, wait in the sand or earth until the weather is right for them to start to grow. While they are waiting, we say they are dormant.

Potatoes grow to their full size and then lie dormant underground until spring, when a new potato plant starts to grow.

 Some mosquitos lay their eggs in mud. The larvae will not hatch until it rains and the mud becomes a pool for them to swim in.

Flower seeds can lie dormant in desert sands for a long time. They only grow when the rain comes.

Glossary

Aestivation

In the summer, when there is very little water, some animals go into a long sleep. This summer sleep is called aestivation.

Learn more about aestivation on pages 26-27.

Bulbs

A bulb is the special underground part of certain plants. The plant stores its food in the bulb and new shoots grow from there.

Learn about bulbs on pages 28-29.

Chlorophyll

Chlorophyll is the green colour in plants. Plants use chlorophyll to make food from sunlight.

See how chlorophyll breaks down in autumn leaves on pages 22-23.

Collection

You can make a collection of all kinds of things that interest you, such as stamps, shells or autographs. For a nature collection, you must only collect things you find on the ground – don't pick flowers or leaves from plants.

Find out how to make a mini museum with a collection of natural things on pages 18-19.

Countryside

The countryside is the fields, woods and hills away from towns and cities. It is a good place to find wild plants and animals.

Learn how to make a nature diary in the city or countryside on pages 6-7.

Dormant

When things are dormant, they are alive but have stopped growing. They wait until the weather is right for them to grow again.

Learn about dormant tubers, eggs and seeds on pages 28-29.

Evergreen trees

Evergreen trees keep their leaves all the year round. Their leaves can be tough and shiny or like thin needles.

Learn more about the leaves you can find in winter on pages 22-23.

Herbs

Herbs are plants that have a strong smell and taste in their stems and leaves. We use herbs for cooking, making herbal teas and even for treating illnesses.

See how you can grow your own herbs in a window box on pages 10-11.

Hibernation

In the winter when there is little food about, some animals save energy by going into a long sleep called hibernation.

Find out how to make a winter shelter for hibernating animals on pages 26-27.

Migration

Migration is the name for the long journey that animals, birds and insects make in order to look for food.

Find out about some amazing journeys on pages 24-25.

Thermometer

A thermometer is an instrument for measuring how hot or cold things are.

Use a thermometer for your nature diary on pages 6-7.

Index